Animals in Danger

BLACK RHINO

Rod Theodorou

Heinemann
LIBRARY

www.heinemann.co.uk

Visit our website to find out more information about Heinemann Library books.

To order:

☎ Phone 44 (0) 1865 888066

🖹 Send a fax to 44 (0) 1865 314091

💻 Visit the Heinemann Bookshop at www.heinemann.co.uk to browse our catalogue and order online.

First published in Great Britain by Heinemann Library,
Halley Court, Jordan Hill, Oxford OX2 8EJ,
a division of Reed Educational and Professional Publishing Ltd.

Heinemann is a registered trademark of Reed Educational and Professional Publishing Ltd.

OXFORD MELBOURNE AUCKLAND
JOHANNESBURG BLANTYRE GABORONE
IBADAN PORTSMOUTH (NH) USA CHICAGO

Designed by Ron Kamen
Illustrated by Dewi Morris/Robert Sydenham
Originated by Ambassador Litho ltd
Printed by South China Printing in Hong Kong/China

ISBN 0 431 13343 3 (hardback)
05 04 03 02 01
10 9 8 7 6 5 4 3 2 1

ISBN 0 431 13348 4 (paperback)
05 04 03 02 01
10 9 8 7 6 5 4 3 2 1

British Library Cataloguing in Publication Data

Theodorou, Rod
  Black rhino. – (Animals in danger) (Take-off!)
  1.Black rhinoceros – Juvenile literature
  2.Endangered species – Juvenile literature
  I.Title
  599.6'68

Acknowledgements

The publishers would like to thank the following for permission to reproduce photographs:
Ardea London: pg.13, RF Porter pg.23; Corbis: pg.11; FLPA: Gerard Lacz pg.4, David Hosking pg.5, pg.22, W Wisniewski pg.6, Eichhorn Zingel pg.8, Frants Hartmann pg.19, pg.21; Mike Johnson: pg.4; NHPA: Martin Harvey pg.18, Daryl Balfour pg.25; Oxford Scientific Films: pg.16, Daniel J Cox pg.4, Tom Leach pg.7, pg.9, Stan Osolonski pg.12, Konrad Wothe pg.14, Steve Turner pg.15, pg.24, David Cayless pg.20; Still Pictures: M & C Denis-Huot pg.17, Michel Gunther pg.26, Roland Seitre pg.27

Cover photograph reproduced with permission of FLPA.

Our thanks to Sue Graves and Hilda Reed for their advice and expertise in the preparation of this book.

Every effort has been made to contact copyright holders of any material reproduced in this book. Any omissions will be rectified in subsequent printings if notice is given to the publishers.

Contents

Any words appearing in the text in bold, **like this**, are explained in the Glossary.

Animals in danger

blue whale

Florida manatee

Bengal tiger

All these animals are in danger.

All over the world, more than 10,000 animal **species** are in danger. Some are in danger because their home is being **destroyed**. Many are in danger because people hunt them.

Black rhinos like this one are in danger of becoming extinct.

This book is about black rhinos and why they are in danger. Black rhinos will become **extinct** if people don't look after them.

5

What is a rhino?

A white rhino, one of the largest rhino species.

Rhinos are huge **mammals**. There are five different **species** of rhino. The two largest species are the black rhino and the white rhino.

A black rhino stands about 1.5 metres high.

horns

A black rhino.

pointed, hooked lip

Black and white rhinos are both grey in colour.
White rhinos have wide, square lips. Black rhinos
have a pointed, hooked lip like a parrot's beak.

What does a rhino look like?

thick, grey skin

huge body

short, thick legs

Rhinos are huge, heavy animals.

Rhinos have huge bodies with thick, grey skin like **armour**. They have short, thick legs with three stumpy toes on each. They are heavy but they can move quickly.

8

The black rhino can weigh up to 1500 kilograms. That is as heavy as a family car!

horns

The black rhino has two horns.

Some rhinos have only one horn. The black rhino has two horns. They are very hard and are used to protect the rhino from **predators**.

Rhino horns are made up of lots of thick hairs pressed tightly together. A black rhino's horn can be over 1 metre long.

Where do rhinos live?

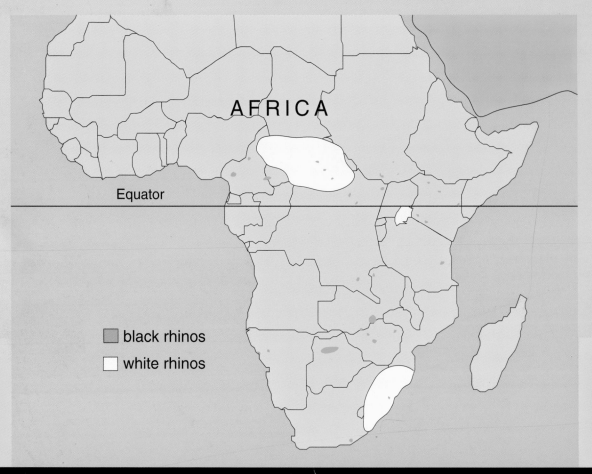

Look at this map of Africa to find out where black and white rhinos live.

Black rhinos and white rhinos both live in Africa. White rhinos like open **savannah** where they can munch away on grass. Black rhinos like to live on the edge of forests amongst bushes and trees.

This Indian rhino is wallowing in a muddy swamp.

Rhinos also live in India, Java and Sumatra. In Java and Sumatra they live deep inside thick **rainforests** where they can eat leaves and fruit. The Indian rhino likes wallowing in cool, muddy swamps and marshes.

11

What do black rhinos eat?

The black rhino uses its hooked lip to pluck off leaves.

Rhinos only eat plants and fruits. Black rhinos use their hooked lip to pluck off leaves or pull down small trees to eat the fruit.

Black rhinos are known as **browsing animals** because they feed on all sorts of different plants.

The black rhino likes to find a shady place to rest.

Black rhinos feed in the morning and late into the
evening. They try to find a shady place to rest
during the hottest part of the day because they do
not like very hot sun.

Black rhino babies

male rhino

female rhino

Black rhinos like to live on their own until it is time to mate.

Black rhinos do not live in family groups. They only come together to **mate**. After mating, the **male** leaves. He does not help to look after the baby.

Several rhinos may be found together in places where there is a good food supply.

calf

mother rhino

The calf can stand one hour after it is born.

The **female** usually only has one baby. The baby is called a calf. The calf can stand up about an hour after it is born. It feeds on its mother's milk.

15

Looking after the calf

calf

horn bump

The calf only has a small bump for a horn.

The calf only has a small bump for a horn, but it grows quickly. It will live with its mother for two or three years. After this time it is big enough to look after itself and live on its own.

Hyenas and lions sometimes attack baby black rhinos. The mother will charge at any **predator** that comes near her calf. Black rhinos can be very fierce if they feel they or their babies are in danger.

A rhino can charge at up to 40 kilometres an hour! That is as fast as a car driving through a town.

17

Unusual rhino facts

ears

eyelashes

Rhinos have eyelashes, and hair at the tips of their ears and tails.

eyes

A black rhino:

- cannot see very well

- has a good sense of smell

- can be dangerous

- usually lives alone.

White rhinos live in groups called herds.

A white rhino:

- cannot see very well
- has a good sense of smell
- is not very dangerous
- lives in a **herd**.

19

How many black rhinos are there?

There are very few black rhinos living in the wild now.

One hundred years ago there were about one million black rhinos in Africa. Now there are fewer than 1900 of them in the wild, even though they are **protected by law**.

This is the **skeleton** of a black rhino.

Black rhinos are being killed faster than any other large animal on Earth. In the last 30 years, **poachers** have killed nearly all the black rhinos in Africa.

Over 73,000 black rhinos have been killed in the last 30 years.

21

Why is the black rhino in danger?

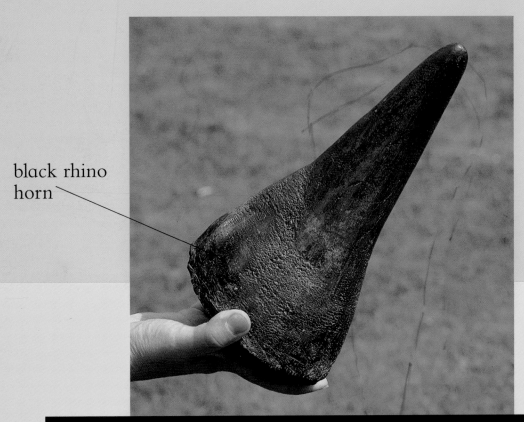

black rhino horn

Hunters shoot black rhinos and cut off their horns to sell them.

Black rhinos are in danger because people shoot them and then cut off their horns to sell. Many horns go to China to be **ground** down and sold as medicine.

horn
handle

daggers

These dagger handles are made of black rhino horn.

Many horns are sold to a country called Yemen in the Middle East. There they are made into the handles of **daggers**.

Even rhino blood and hooves are used in some medicines that are sold in Asia.

23

How is the black rhino being helped?

This black rhino has its own guard to protect it from hunters.

Many leaders in China and Yemen are trying to stop people selling rhino horn. All African and Asian countries have made **laws** to stop people hunting rhinos.

These conservation workers are looking after two black rhinos whose mothers were killed.

Conservation groups like the World Wide Fund for Nature (WWF) are also working to stop **poachers** and save the rhino.

In some countries black rhinos are caught and their horns are cut off and burned. This stops **poachers** killing them to get their horns. The horns then grow back.

The rhino does not feel pain when its horn is cut off. It's a bit like when you have your hair or nails cut.

guard

Some black rhinos live in protected places like this.

Many African countries have places where the rhinos are **protected** by fences and guards. This is the best way to save the black rhino. The safe area is quite large so the rhinos can wander about freely.

27

Black rhino factfile

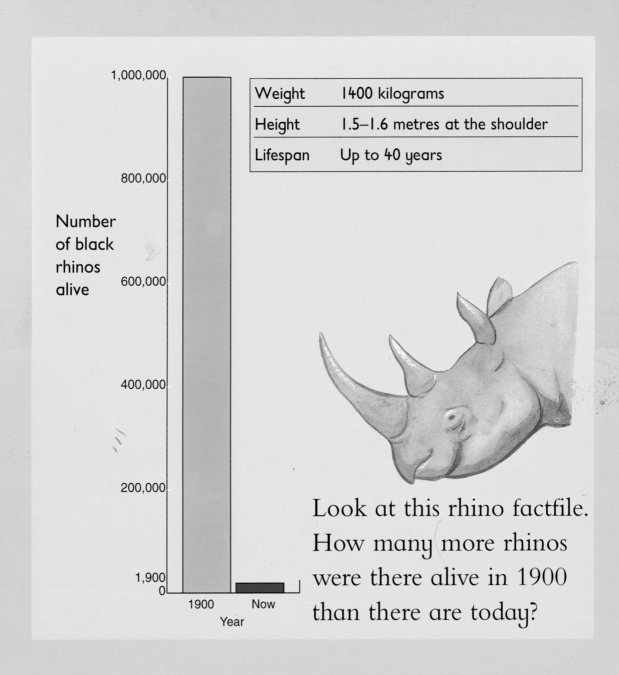

Weight	1400 kilograms
Height	1.5–1.6 metres at the shoulder
Lifespan	Up to 40 years

Number of black rhinos alive

1,000,000

800,000

600,000

400,000

200,000

1,900
0

1900   Now

Year

Look at this rhino factfile. How many more rhinos were there alive in 1900 than there are today?

World danger table

	Number that may have been alive 100 years ago	Number that may be alive today
Giant panda	65,000	650
Bengal tiger	100,000	4500
Blue whale	335,000	4000
Mountain gorilla	85,000	500
Florida manatee	75,000	1400

There are thousands of other animals in the world that are in danger of becoming **extinct**. This table shows some of these animals.

How can you find out more about them?

Further reading, addresses and websites

Books

Rhinoceroses, Endangered! series, Amanda Harman, Benchmark Books, Marshall Cavendish, 1997

Rhino, Caroline Arnold, Morrow Junior Books, 1995

Rhinos, Wildlife at Risk series, Malcolm Penny, Wayland, 1991

The African Rhino, Animals in Danger series, William R. Sanford and Carl R. Green, Heinemann, 1990

Vanishing Species, Green Issues series, Miles Barton, Franklin Watts, 1997

Organizations

Friends of the Earth:
UK – 26–28 Underwood Street, London N1 7JQ ☎ (020) 7490 1555
Australia – 312 Smith Street, Collingwood, Vic 3065 ☎ 03 9419 8700

Greenpeace:
UK – Canonbury Villas, London N1 2PN ☎ (020) 7865 8100
Australia – Level 4, 39 Liverpool Street, Sydney, NSW 2000 ☎ 02 9261 4666

WWF:
UK – Panda House, Weyside Park, Catteshall Lane, Godalming, Surrey GU7 1XR ☎ (01483) 426 444
Australia – Level 5, 725 George Street, Sydney, NSW 2000 ☎ 02 9281 5515

Useful websites

www.bbc.net
The BBC's animals site. Go to Animal Zone for information on all sorts of animals, including fun activities, the latest news, and links to programmes.

www.defenders.org
The site of a conservation group dedicated to protecting animals and plants. Go to Kids Planet on their site.

www.rhinos-irf.org
The International Rhino Foundation's site, dedicated to the conservation of the rhino.

www.sandiegozoo.org
The world-famous American San Diego Zoo's site. Go to the Pick an Animal section for games and factsheets.

www.wwf.org
The site of the World Wide Fund for Nature (WWF), the world's largest independent conservation organization. The WWF conserves wildlife and the natural environment for present and future generations.

Glossary

armour	strong layer that protects, like a suit of metal
browsing animal	animal that feeds on leaves, shoots and the bark of trees and bushes
conservation	looking after animals, places or things so that they can continue to exist
dagger	a sharp, pointed knife with a handle
destroyed	spoilt, broken or torn apart so it can not be used
extinct	completely died out and can never live again
female	the opposite of a male, such as a girl or woman
ground	crushed into powder
herd	group of the same animals living together
law	rule or something you have to do
male	the opposite of a female, such as a boy or a man
mammals	warm-blooded animals, like humans, that feed on their mother's milk when they are young
mate	when a male animal and a female animal come together to make baby animals
poachers	hunters who make money from hunting animals to sell parts of their bodies like teeth, bones and fur
predator	animal that hunts and kills other animals
protected	looked after, sometimes by law
protected by law	there are laws to make sure they are not harmed
rainforest	tropical forest that is very hot and damp
savannah	large areas of grassland with few trees
skeleton	the frames of bones in animals and humans
species	a group of living things that are very similar

Index

Titles in the *Animals in Danger* series include:

Hardback   0 431 13342 5

Hardback   0 431 13343 3

Hardback   0 431 13341 7

Hardback   0 431 13340 9

Find out about the other titles in this series on our website www.heinemann.co.uk/library